I wonder what life would be like if we believed in ourselves more than we doubted ourselves...

I wonder...

Welcome!

Fear. Oh how one emotion can control and restrict everything.

How often have you…

- Been scared to raise your prices incase no one will hire you anymore.
- Wanted to change careers but not quite taken the leap in case it doesn't work out.
- Let a boundary that's important to you slip because you were afraid if you spoke up you'd upset or lose a client.
- Turned down an exciting opportunity because you felt like you weren't 'ready yet'.
- Put off launching a new product or service because a little voice said… 'You're not good enough. It's not good enough. No one's going to want to buy THAT…'

So you stay safe, stuck, doing the exact same thing day after day after day… Whether it makes you happy or not.

When I ask my clients - honestly - what's really stopping them or getting in the way of them doing of them doing something they really want, every single time I get the same answer…

A quiet… **"Me."**

When they say 'me' what I really know they mean of course is Fear.

The scared voice we all have inside of us yet the voice that only some have learnt to make friends with and work with so that it no longer is the voice that stops them from living the life they want or achieving all they're truly capable of.

Through The Daily Brave I'm going to share with you my favourite simple yet powerful exercise that'll help you overcome fear and self doubt in any situation so it never holds you back or stops you again.

To being, doing and achieving EVERYTHING you want in this life.

You've got this,

Ruth xo

Fear, and why we have it

In a nutshell Fear has one job - to keep us safe.

We may hate being scared sometimes (understandably) but Fear is doing a super valuable job (again, keeping - or at least trying to keep - us safe) that of course we all totally need. The only problem comes however when Fear gets a little too over excited and tries to protect us from every. little. thing. that it sees as new or different (Fear REALLY hates change or anything it sees as outside of its 'comfort zone').

So when Fear does get nervous or scared it starts trying to get its point across and protect us by talking REALLY LOUDLY, and if we don't listen the first time (by either stopping or getting away from the thing that's scaring it) then it talks louder and louder and LOUDER until we do - sometimes to the point where it even SHOUTS AT US (which is always, erm... 'Fun').

So instead of trying to quieten Fear or pretend it's not there, The Daily Brave exercise is not only one that allows Fear to be fully seen and heard (so it can stop shouting at you!) but also one that'll allow you to tap into other voices that you have within you (Belief, Curiosity, Courage and Love) that are far more loving and supportive in wanting to see you succeed at every single dream you have - even the big scary ones.

Think of it this way...

Imagine you're sat in a car and Fear is right up there in the drivers seat. It has control of the wheel (which direction you go) and both the accelerator and brake (how fast - or not - you get there).

Is fear gunna drive you in the direction of your biggest, wildest, craziest dream? Erm, no. It's gunna firmly out it's foot on the brake, turn off the engine and take the keys out of the ignition so you stay put and don't go anywhere at all.

That or it'll start driving you straight back in the direction you've already come to a place it knows and feels safe, even if that place is somewhere you felt miserable and unhappy.

To Fear you can be as unhappy as you want (it really doesn't care) because as long as you're 'safe'... Well it's then done its job.

However put someone else in the drivers seat, say Belief, well where do you think it's going to drive you? The same direction as Fear? No way. It's likely going to drive you in the opposite direction, to the place that feels exciting and you and that it knows you're totally capable of reaching/doing/achieving because it believes in you.

Likewise Curiosity, Courage and Love... Which direction will each of them likely drive you in?

Would they slam on the brakes keeping you exactly where you are or would they put their foot on the accelerator and say... 'Woohoo let's go!'

So that is exactly what we're going to do...

How to use this journal

Over the next 222 pages you'll see six prompts :

1. What's happening...

In this section each time you feel nervous, scared, or that you're doubting yourself or a decision you need to make, write down what's happening that's making Fear to speak up.

For example :

- You're launching a new online course and you're worried whether or not it's good enough or whether anyone will buy it.
- You need to give a speech and are worried about messing up, stumbling over your words or forgetting pretty much everything you've got planned to say.
- You need to say no to someone and you don't know how they're going to take it.

Whatever it is that's going on for you right now and bringing up a feeling of either fear or doubt, write it down in this section.

2. Fear, what do you have to say?

While normally most of us try and stick our fingers in our ears while singing 'La la la la laaaaaaaaaaa' to drown out whatever Fear has to say to us so we can push on through...

Here you're going to do the opposite, because here you're going to give Fear the space to be fully heard, seen and listened to.

In this section ask Fear what is has to say about the situation and write it down - and keep going and going and going until it's done. You want fear to be so seen and heard that it has nothing left to say.

Now as a heads up the first time you do this exercise it'll likely have A LOT to say. Actually it probably will the first few times you do this exercise as it'll be like… "Hurrah! She's finally listening to me, so…" (rolls out very very VERY long list).

This by the way is totally normal so embrace away. The good news however is that the more you do this exercise the less Fear will have to say as it won't feel like it needs to repeat itself over and over and over again (or shout!) to be fully heard each time. Knowing you're giving Fear the full space it wants to be heard is often enough.

So when you write down what it has to say before moving on just check in with Fear again and say something like…

"Thanks Fear. Is there anything else you want to say?"

Again at the start it'll usually be like "Yup!" and off it'll go again.

Whatever it is write it all down and keep asking Fear until finally it says… "Nope, I'm good, I'm done now, I just wanted to make sure you heard me..."

For me I then say one final thanks to Fear for letting me know what it had to say before then moving on to ask...

3. Belief, what do you have to say?

Now again the first time you go through this practice it's likely fear will talk VERY LOUDLY and talk A LOT - especially if you've been trying to suppress it for a while.

However on the flip side it's likely that Belief will be the opposite - quite quiet and timid, and to begin with you might have to REALLY listen to it as it whispers away in order to hear it.

Why? Because Belief is often used to being shot down by Fear every time it speaks up so it also needs to get used to knowing that it's ok for it to have a voice and be heard too and that you're going to give it just as much love and space and Fear to be fully heard and seen.

So just like with Fear you're going to ask Belief... "What do you have to say?" - and write that down too.

And again just like Fear you're going to say... "Thanks Belief, is there anything else you want to say?" - and keep going until Belief too is like, "Nope, I'm good thank you..." and it feels fully heard and seen too.

Once done then it's time to move onto...

4. Curiosity, what do you have to say?

Now personally I LOVE asking Curiosity what it has to say and bring to the table. You wanna know why? Because Curiosity usually says something like...

"Ridgeway, you're doing that assuming thing again where you think everything's gunna go wrong but you don't KNOW that. Instead of assuming can we just go and try it and see what happens instead?"

Curiosity makes something 'click' in my brain and reminds me that sure whatever it is that I'm doing might not go well, or of course it might, or on the other hand it might go somewhere completely in the middle (which is usually does) so ummmm hello, how about we do just see?!

#PointWellMadeCuriosity

So just Like Fear and Belief you're going to check in with Curiosity and ask it what it has to say before writing it all down too.

Then once Curiosity has been fully heard it's time to ask...

5. Courage, what do you have to say?

For me I find Courage is pretty straight to the point and it usually says something like...

"Screw it, if you're game I'm TOTALLY game. When do we get started?!"

Use this space to write down everything Courage has to say to you before finally then asking...

6. Love, what do you have to say?

Ahhh the most beautiful voice of all that always knows just the most perfect and right and loving (of course!) thing to say.

When you've checked in with all the other voices, lastly ask Love what it wants to say.

I remember the first time I did this exercise when I was feeling really nervous about something and Love quite simply said...

"I've got you. No matter what happens I'm going to love you and be here for you."

In that instant I knew that no matter what did happen - I'd be ok.

While Fear was trying to scare me Love gave me the biggest, safest, most loving hug right when I needed it. I knew I had me and that while Fear was still going to be there I also knew that everything was going to be ok because Love was right there with me (no matter what) too.

Enjoy this section, it really is a beautiful one.

Most of all know The Daily Brave isn't about removing Fear altogether but allowing it to be ONE voice in the conversation. To sure do its job but no more or less than any of the other voices within you to do theirs (lovingly) too.

Reflection pages

After every five page spread you'll also find a reflection page.

While it's powerful to go through The Daily Brave practice when you're feeling fear or doubt, it's also powerful to take a few minutes outside of those big times and emotions when you're not deep in the thick of things to reflect on what you've learnt so far over the past few times you've gone through the exercise.

If you get stuck on where to begin these are great prompts to start with :

What has Fear taught you?

What has Belief taught you?

What has Curiosity taught you?

What has Courage taught you?

What has Love taught you?

Ps...

You're welcome to keep your journal entries to yourself (of course!), however if you'd like to share any or follow along with some of mine or others who are going through this journal, you're welcome to use the hashtag **#RUTHXO**.

You'll also find me on Instagram at **@ruthridgewayxo.**

And online at **www.ruthxo.com.**

What's happening...

Fear, what do you have to say?

Belief, what do you have to say?

Curiosity, what do you have to say?

_____
_____
_____
_____
_____
_____

Courage, what do you have to say?

_____
_____
_____
_____
_____
_____

Love, what do you have to say?

_____
_____
_____
_____
_____
_____

DATE : _____

What's happening...

Fear, what do you have to say?

Belief, what do you have to say?

Curiosity, what do you have to say?

_____
_____
_____
_____
_____

Courage, what do you have to say?

_____
_____
_____
_____
_____

Love, what do you have to say?

_____
_____
_____
_____
_____

DATE : _____

What's happening...

Fear, what do you have to say?

Belief, what do you have to say?

Curiosity, what do you have to say?

Courage, what do you have to say?

Love, what do you have to say?

DATE : _____

What's happening...

Fear, what do you have to say?

Belief, what do you have to say?

Curiosity, what do you have to say?

_____
_____
_____
_____
_____

Courage, what do you have to say?

_____
_____
_____
_____
_____

Love, what do you have to say?

_____
_____
_____
_____
_____

DATE : _____

What's happening...

Fear, what do you have to say?

Belief, what do you have to say?

Curiosity, what do you have to say?

_____
_____
_____
_____
_____
_____

Courage, what do you have to say?

_____
_____
_____
_____
_____
_____

Love, what do you have to say?

_____
_____
_____
_____
_____
_____

DATE : _____

I love myself enough to...
Believe in myself more than I doubt myself.

Reflections...

DATE : _____

What's happening...

Fear, what do you have to say?

Belief, what do you have to say?

Curiosity, what do you have to say?

Courage, what do you have to say?

Love, what do you have to say?

DATE : _____

What's happening...

Fear, what do you have to say?

Belief, what do you have to say?

Curiosity, what do you have to say?

Courage, what do you have to say?

Love, what do you have to say?

DATE : _____

What's happening...

Fear, what do you have to say?

Belief, what do you have to say?

Curiosity, what do you have to say?

Courage, what do you have to say?

Love, what do you have to say?

DATE : _____

What's happening...

Fear, what do you have to say?

Belief, what do you have to say?

Curiosity, what do you have to say?

___

Courage, what do you have to say?

___

Love, what do you have to say?

___

DATE : _____

What's happening...

Fear, what do you have to say?

Belief, what do you have to say?

Curiosity, what do you have to say?

_____
_____
_____
_____
_____
_____

Courage, what do you have to say?

_____
_____
_____
_____
_____
_____

Love, what do you have to say?

_____
_____
_____
_____
_____
_____

DATE : _____

I love myself enough to...
Be courageous even when scared.

Reflections...

DATE : _____

What's happening...

Fear, what do you have to say?

Belief, what do you have to say?

Curiosity, what do you have to say?

_____
_____
_____
_____
_____

Courage, what do you have to say?

_____
_____
_____
_____
_____

Love, what do you have to say?

_____
_____
_____
_____
_____

DATE : _____

What's happening...

Fear, what do you have to say?

Belief, what do you have to say?

Curiosity, what do you have to say?

_____
_____
_____
_____
_____

Courage, what do you have to say?

_____
_____
_____
_____
_____

Love, what do you have to say?

_____
_____
_____
_____
_____

DATE : _____

What's happening...

Fear, what do you have to say?

Belief, what do you have to say?

Curiosity, what do you have to say?

_____
_____
_____
_____
_____
_____

Courage, what do you have to say?

_____
_____
_____
_____
_____
_____

Love, what do you have to say?

_____
_____
_____
_____
_____
_____

DATE : _____

What's happening...

Fear, what do you have to say?

Belief, what do you have to say?

Curiosity, what do you have to say?

Courage, what do you have to say?

Love, what do you have to say?

DATE : _____

What's happening...

Fear, what do you have to say?

Belief, what do you have to say?

Curiosity, what do you have to say?

Courage, what do you have to say?

Love, what do you have to say?

DATE : _____

I love myself enough to...
Be brave in asking for what I *really* want.

Reflections...

DATE : _____

What's happening...

Fear, what do you have to say?

Belief, what do you have to say?

Curiosity, what do you have to say?

Courage, what do you have to say?

Love, what do you have to say?

DATE : _____

What's happening...

Fear, what do you have to say?

Belief, what do you have to say?

Curiosity, what do you have to say?

_____
_____
_____
_____
_____
_____

Courage, what do you have to say?

_____
_____
_____
_____
_____
_____

Love, what do you have to say?

_____
_____
_____
_____
_____
_____

DATE : _____

What's happening...

Fear, what do you have to say?

Belief, what do you have to say?

Curiosity, what do you have to say?

Courage, what do you have to say?

Love, what do you have to say?

DATE : _____

What's happening...

Fear, what do you have to say?

Belief, what do you have to say?

Curiosity, what do you have to say?

Courage, what do you have to say?

Love, what do you have to say?

DATE : _____

What's happening...

Fear, what do you have to say?

Belief, what do you have to say?

Curiosity, what do you have to say?

_____
_____
_____
_____
_____
_____

Courage, what do you have to say?

_____
_____
_____
_____
_____
_____

Love, what do you have to say?

_____
_____
_____
_____
_____
_____

DATE : _____

I love myself enough to...
Love all of me.

Reflections...

DATE : _____

What's happening...

Fear, what do you have to say?

Belief, what do you have to say?

Curiosity, what do you have to say?

Courage, what do you have to say?

Love, what do you have to say?

DATE : _____

What's happening...

Fear, what do you have to say?

Belief, what do you have to say?

Curiosity, what do you have to say?

Courage, what do you have to say?

Love, what do you have to say?

DATE : _____

What's happening...

Fear, what do you have to say?

Belief, what do you have to say?

Curiosity, what do you have to say?

_____
_____
_____
_____
_____

Courage, what do you have to say?

_____
_____
_____
_____
_____

Love, what do you have to say?

_____
_____
_____
_____
_____

DATE : _____

What's happening...

Fear, what do you have to say?

Belief, what do you have to say?

Curiosity, what do you have to say?

_____
_____
_____
_____
_____

Courage, what do you have to say?

_____
_____
_____
_____
_____

Love, what do you have to say?

_____
_____
_____
_____
_____

DATE : _____

What's happening...

Fear, what do you have to say?

Belief, what do you have to say?

Curiosity, what do you have to say?

Courage, what do you have to say?

Love, what do you have to say?

DATE : _____

I love myself enough to...
Not let my fears define me.

Reflections...

DATE : _____

What's happening...

Fear, what do you have to say?

Belief, what do you have to say?

Curiosity, what do you have to say?

_____
_____
_____
_____
_____

Courage, what do you have to say?

_____
_____
_____
_____
_____

Love, what do you have to say?

_____
_____
_____
_____
_____

DATE : _____

What's happening...

Fear, what do you have to say?

Belief, what do you have to say?

Curiosity, what do you have to say?

Courage, what do you have to say?

Love, what do you have to say?

DATE : _____

What's happening...

Fear, what do you have to say?

Belief, what do you have to say?

Curiosity, what do you have to say?

_____
_____
_____
_____
_____
_____

Courage, what do you have to say?

_____
_____
_____
_____
_____
_____

Love, what do you have to say?

_____
_____
_____
_____
_____
_____

DATE : _____

What's happening...

Fear, what do you have to say?

Belief, what do you have to say?

Curiosity, what do you have to say?

Courage, what do you have to say?

Love, what do you have to say?

DATE : _____

What's happening...

_____
_____
_____
_____
_____

Fear, what do you have to say?

_____
_____
_____
_____
_____

Belief, what do you have to say?

_____
_____
_____
_____
_____

Curiosity, what do you have to say?

_____
_____
_____
_____
_____

Courage, what do you have to say?

_____
_____
_____
_____
_____

Love, what do you have to say?

_____
_____
_____
_____
_____

DATE : _____

I love myself enough to...
Stop comparing myself to others.

Reflections...

DATE : _____

What's happening...

Fear, what do you have to say?

Belief, what do you have to say?

Curiosity, what do you have to say?

Courage, what do you have to say?

Love, what do you have to say?

DATE : _____

What's happening...

Fear, what do you have to say?

Belief, what do you have to say?

Curiosity, what do you have to say?

_____
_____
_____
_____
_____

Courage, what do you have to say?

_____
_____
_____
_____
_____

Love, what do you have to say?

_____
_____
_____
_____
_____

DATE : _____

What's happening...

Fear, what do you have to say?

Belief, what do you have to say?

Curiosity, what do you have to say?

Courage, what do you have to say?

Love, what do you have to say?

DATE : _____

What's happening...

Fear, what do you have to say?

Belief, what do you have to say?

Curiosity, what do you have to say?

Courage, what do you have to say?

Love, what do you have to say?

DATE : _____

What's happening...

Fear, what do you have to say?

Belief, what do you have to say?

Curiosity, what do you have to say?

_____
_____
_____
_____
_____

Courage, what do you have to say?

_____
_____
_____
_____
_____

Love, what do you have to say?

_____
_____
_____
_____
_____

DATE : _____

I love myself enough to... **Believe in myself today.**

Reflections...

DATE : _____

What's happening...

Fear, what do you have to say?

Belief, what do you have to say?

Curiosity, what do you have to say?

_____
_____
_____
_____
_____
_____

Courage, what do you have to say?

_____
_____
_____
_____
_____
_____

Love, what do you have to say?

_____
_____
_____
_____
_____
_____

DATE : _____

What's happening...

Fear, what do you have to say?

Belief, what do you have to say?

Curiosity, what do you have to say?

Courage, what do you have to say?

Love, what do you have to say?

DATE : _____

What's happening...

Fear, what do you have to say?

Belief, what do you have to say?

Curiosity, what do you have to say?

Courage, what do you have to say?

Love, what do you have to say?

DATE : _____

What's happening...

Fear, what do you have to say?

Belief, what do you have to say?

Curiosity, what do you have to say?

_____
_____
_____
_____
_____
_____

Courage, what do you have to say?

_____
_____
_____
_____
_____
_____

Love, what do you have to say?

_____
_____
_____
_____
_____
_____

DATE : _____

What's happening...

Fear, what do you have to say?

Belief, what do you have to say?

Curiosity, what do you have to say?

_____
_____
_____
_____
_____
_____

Courage, what do you have to say?

_____
_____
_____
_____
_____
_____

Love, what do you have to say?

_____
_____
_____
_____
_____
_____

DATE : _____

Repeat :
I can do this.
I can do this.
I can do this.

Reflections...

DATE : _____

What's happening...

Fear, what do you have to say?

Belief, what do you have to say?

Curiosity, what do you have to say?

Courage, what do you have to say?

Love, what do you have to say?

DATE : _____

What's happening...

Fear, what do you have to say?

Belief, what do you have to say?

Curiosity, what do you have to say?

Courage, what do you have to say?

Love, what do you have to say?

DATE : _____

What's happening...

Fear, what do you have to say?

Belief, what do you have to say?

Curiosity, what do you have to say?

_____
_____
_____
_____
_____
_____

Courage, what do you have to say?

_____
_____
_____
_____
_____
_____

Love, what do you have to say?

_____
_____
_____
_____
_____
_____

DATE : _____

What's happening...

Fear, what do you have to say?

Belief, what do you have to say?

Curiosity, what do you have to say?

Courage, what do you have to say?

Love, what do you have to say?

DATE : _____

What's happening...

Fear, what do you have to say?

Belief, what do you have to say?

Curiosity, what do you have to say?

_____
_____
_____
_____
_____
_____

Courage, what do you have to say?

_____
_____
_____
_____
_____
_____

Love, what do you have to say?

_____
_____
_____
_____
_____
_____

DATE : _____

I love myself enough to...
No longer play smaller than what I'm really capable of.

Reflections...

DATE : _____

What's happening...

Fear, what do you have to say?

Belief, what do you have to say?

Curiosity, what do you have to say?

_____
_____
_____
_____
_____
_____

Courage, what do you have to say?

_____
_____
_____
_____
_____
_____

Love, what do you have to say?

_____
_____
_____
_____
_____
_____

DATE : _____

What's happening...

Fear, what do you have to say?

Belief, what do you have to say?

Curiosity, what do you have to say?

_____
_____
_____
_____
_____
_____

Courage, what do you have to say?

_____
_____
_____
_____
_____
_____

Love, what do you have to say?

_____
_____
_____
_____
_____
_____

DATE : _____

What's happening...

Fear, what do you have to say?

Belief, what do you have to say?

Curiosity, what do you have to say?

_____
_____
_____
_____
_____

Courage, what do you have to say?

_____
_____
_____
_____
_____

Love, what do you have to say?

_____
_____
_____
_____
_____

DATE : _____

What's happening...

_____
_____
_____
_____
_____

Fear, what do you have to say?

_____
_____
_____
_____
_____

Belief, what do you have to say?

_____
_____
_____
_____
_____

Curiosity, what do you have to say?

_____

_____

_____

_____

_____

Courage, what do you have to say?

_____

_____

_____

_____

_____

Love, what do you have to say?

_____

_____

_____

_____

_____

DATE : _____

What's happening...

Fear, what do you have to say?

Belief, what do you have to say?

Curiosity, what do you have to say?

Courage, what do you have to say?

Love, what do you have to say?

DATE : _____

I love myself enough to... **Go after my biggest, wildest, craziest dreams.**

Reflections...

DATE: _____

What's happening...

Fear, what do you have to say?

Belief, what do you have to say?

Curiosity, what do you have to say?

Courage, what do you have to say?

Love, what do you have to say?

DATE : _____

What's happening...

Fear, what do you have to say?

Belief, what do you have to say?

Curiosity, what do you have to say?

Courage, what do you have to say?

Love, what do you have to say?

DATE : _____

What's happening...

Fear, what do you have to say?

Belief, what do you have to say?

Curiosity, what do you have to say?

_____
_____
_____
_____
_____
_____

Courage, what do you have to say?

_____
_____
_____
_____
_____
_____

Love, what do you have to say?

_____
_____
_____
_____
_____
_____

DATE : _____

What's happening...

Fear, what do you have to say?

Belief, what do you have to say?

Curiosity, what do you have to say?

Courage, what do you have to say?

Love, what do you have to say?

DATE : _____

What's happening...

Fear, what do you have to say?

Belief, what do you have to say?

Curiosity, what do you have to say?

___

Courage, what do you have to say?

___

Love, what do you have to say?

___

DATE : _____

I love myself enough to...
Try.

Reflections...

DATE : _____

What's happening...

Fear, what do you have to say?

Belief, what do you have to say?

What's happening...

Fear, what do you have to say?

Belief, what do you have to say?

Curiosity, what do you have to say?

_____
_____
_____
_____
_____

Courage, what do you have to say?

_____
_____
_____
_____
_____

Love, what do you have to say?

_____
_____
_____
_____
_____
_____

DATE : _____

What's happening...

Fear, what do you have to say?

Belief, what do you have to say?

Curiosity, what do you have to say?

_____
_____
_____
_____
_____
_____

Courage, what do you have to say?

_____
_____
_____
_____
_____
_____

Love, what do you have to say?

_____
_____
_____
_____
_____
_____

DATE : _____

Curiosity, what do you have to say?

Courage, what do you have to say?

Love, what do you have to say?

DATE : _____

What's happening...

Fear, what do you have to say?

Belief, what do you have to say?

Curiosity, what do you have to say?

_____
_____
_____
_____
_____

Courage, what do you have to say?

_____
_____
_____
_____
_____

Love, what do you have to say?

_____
_____
_____
_____
_____

DATE : _____

What's happening...

Fear, what do you have to say?

Belief, what do you have to say?

Curiosity, what do you have to say?

Courage, what do you have to say?

Love, what do you have to say?

DATE : _____

I love myself enough to... Become an even better version of myself everyday.

Reflections...

DATE : _____

What's happening...

Fear, what do you have to say?

Belief, what do you have to say?

Curiosity, what do you have to say?

Courage, what do you have to say?

Love, what do you have to say?

DATE : _____

What's happening...

Fear, what do you have to say?

Belief, what do you have to say?

Curiosity, what do you have to say?

Courage, what do you have to say?

Love, what do you have to say?

DATE : _____

What's happening...

Fear, what do you have to say?

Belief, what do you have to say?

Curiosity, what do you have to say?

_____
_____
_____
_____
_____
_____

Courage, what do you have to say?

_____
_____
_____
_____
_____
_____

Love, what do you have to say?

_____
_____
_____
_____
_____
_____

DATE : _____

What's happening...

Fear, what do you have to say?

Belief, what do you have to say?

Curiosity, what do you have to say?

Courage, what do you have to say?

Love, what do you have to say?

DATE : _____

What's happening...

_____
_____
_____
_____
_____

Fear, what do you have to say?

_____
_____
_____
_____
_____

Belief, what do you have to say?

_____
_____
_____
_____
_____

Curiosity, what do you have to say?

Courage, what do you have to say?

Love, what do you have to say?

DATE : _____

I love myself enough to...
Be proud of what I've already achieved.

Reflections...

DATE : _____

What's happening...

Fear, what do you have to say?

Belief, what do you have to say?

Curiosity, what do you have to say?

_____
_____
_____
_____
_____
_____

Courage, what do you have to say?

_____
_____
_____
_____
_____
_____

Love, what do you have to say?

_____
_____
_____
_____
_____
_____

DATE : _____

What's happening...

Fear, what do you have to say?

Belief, what do you have to say?

Curiosity, what do you have to say?

_____
_____
_____
_____
_____
_____

Courage, what do you have to say?

_____
_____
_____
_____
_____
_____

Love, what do you have to say?

_____
_____
_____
_____
_____
_____

DATE : _____

What's happening...

Fear, what do you have to say?

Belief, what do you have to say?

Curiosity, what do you have to say?

Courage, what do you have to say?

Love, what do you have to say?

DATE : _____

What's happening...

Fear, what do you have to say?

Belief, what do you have to say?

Curiosity, what do you have to say?

Courage, what do you have to say?

Love, what do you have to say?

DATE : _____

What's happening...

Fear, what do you have to say?

Belief, what do you have to say?

Curiosity, what do you have to say?

_____
_____
_____
_____
_____
_____

Courage, what do you have to say?

_____
_____
_____
_____
_____
_____

Love, what do you have to say?

_____
_____
_____
_____
_____
_____

DATE : _____

I love myself enough to... **Create the life I really want.**

Reflections...

DATE : _____

What's happening...

Fear, what do you have to say?

Belief, what do you have to say?

Curiosity, what do you have to say?

Courage, what do you have to say?

Love, what do you have to say?

DATE : _____

What's happening...

Fear, what do you have to say?

Belief, what do you have to say?

Curiosity, what do you have to say?

___

Courage, what do you have to say?

___

Love, what do you have to say?

___

DATE : _____

What's happening...

Fear, what do you have to say?

Belief, what do you have to say?

Curiosity, what do you have to say?

Courage, what do you have to say?

Love, what do you have to say?

DATE : _____

What's happening...

_____
_____
_____
_____
_____
_____

Fear, what do you have to say?

_____
_____
_____
_____
_____
_____

Belief, what do you have to say?

_____
_____
_____
_____
_____
_____

Curiosity, what do you have to say?

_____
_____
_____
_____
_____

Courage, what do you have to say?

_____
_____
_____
_____
_____

Love, what do you have to say?

_____
_____
_____
_____
_____

DATE : _____

What's happening...

Fear, what do you have to say?

Belief, what do you have to say?

Curiosity, what do you have to say?

Courage, what do you have to say?

Love, what do you have to say?

DATE : _____

I love myself enough to... **Take action even though I don't have everything figured out yet.**

Reflections...

DATE: _____

What's happening...

Fear, what do you have to say?

Belief, what do you have to say?

Curiosity, what do you have to say?

Courage, what do you have to say?

Love, what do you have to say?

DATE : _____

What's happening...

Fear, what do you have to say?

Belief, what do you have to say?

Curiosity, what do you have to say?

_____
_____
_____
_____
_____
_____

Courage, what do you have to say?

_____
_____
_____
_____
_____
_____

Love, what do you have to say?

_____
_____
_____
_____
_____
_____

DATE : _____

What's happening...

Fear, what do you have to say?

Belief, what do you have to say?

Curiosity, what do you have to say?

Courage, what do you have to say?

Love, what do you have to say?

DATE : _____

What's happening...

Fear, what do you have to say?

Belief, what do you have to say?

Curiosity, what do you have to say?

_____
_____
_____
_____
_____
_____

Courage, what do you have to say?

_____
_____
_____
_____
_____
_____

Love, what do you have to say?

_____
_____
_____
_____
_____
_____

DATE : _____

What's happening...

Fear, what do you have to say?

Belief, what do you have to say?

Curiosity, what do you have to say?

Courage, what do you have to say?

Love, what do you have to say?

DATE : _____

I love myself enough to... Believe in my dreams and that I can achieve anything I want.

Reflections...

DATE : _____

What's happening...

Fear, what do you have to say?

Belief, what do you have to say?

Curiosity, what do you have to say?

Courage, what do you have to say?

Love, what do you have to say?

DATE : _____

What's happening...

Fear, what do you have to say?

Belief, what do you have to say?

Curiosity, what do you have to say?

Courage, what do you have to say?

Love, what do you have to say?

DATE : _____

What's happening...

Fear, what do you have to say?

Belief, what do you have to say?

Curiosity, what do you have to say?

_____
_____
_____
_____
_____
_____

Courage, what do you have to say?

_____
_____
_____
_____
_____
_____

Love, what do you have to say?

_____
_____
_____
_____
_____
_____

DATE : _____

What's happening...

Fear, what do you have to say?

Belief, what do you have to say?

Curiosity, what do you have to say?

_____
_____
_____
_____
_____

Courage, what do you have to say?

_____
_____
_____
_____
_____

Love, what do you have to say?

_____
_____
_____
_____
_____

DATE : _____

What's happening...

Fear, what do you have to say?

Belief, what do you have to say?

Curiosity, what do you have to say?

_____
_____
_____
_____
_____

Courage, what do you have to say?

_____
_____
_____
_____
_____

Love, what do you have to say?

_____
_____
_____
_____
_____

DATE : _____

Repeat:
I am enough.
I am enough.
I am enough.

Reflections...

DATE : _____

What's happening...

Fear, what do you have to say?

Belief, what do you have to say?

Curiosity, what do you have to say?

_____
_____
_____
_____
_____

Courage, what do you have to say?

_____
_____
_____
_____
_____

Love, what do you have to say?

_____
_____
_____
_____
_____

DATE : _____

What's happening...

Fear, what do you have to say?

Belief, what do you have to say?

Curiosity, what do you have to say?

_____
_____
_____
_____
_____
_____

Courage, what do you have to say?

_____
_____
_____
_____
_____
_____

Love, what do you have to say?

_____
_____
_____
_____
_____
_____

DATE : _____

What's happening...

Fear, what do you have to say?

Belief, what do you have to say?

Curiosity, what do you have to say?

Courage, what do you have to say?

Love, what do you have to say?

DATE : _____

What's happening...

Fear, what do you have to say?

Belief, what do you have to say?

Curiosity, what do you have to say?

_____
_____
_____
_____
_____

Courage, what do you have to say?

_____
_____
_____
_____
_____

Love, what do you have to say?

_____
_____
_____
_____
_____

DATE : _____

What's happening...

Fear, what do you have to say?

Belief, what do you have to say?

Curiosity, what do you have to say?

_____
_____
_____
_____
_____

Courage, what do you have to say?

_____
_____
_____
_____
_____

Love, what do you have to say?

_____
_____
_____
_____
_____

DATE : _____

I love myself enough to... Make decisions from a place of love instead of fear.

Reflections...

DATE : _____

What's happening...

Fear, what do you have to say?

Belief, what do you have to say?

Curiosity, what do you have to say?

_____
_____
_____
_____
_____
_____

Courage, what do you have to say?

_____
_____
_____
_____
_____
_____

Love, what do you have to say?

_____
_____
_____
_____
_____
_____

DATE : _____

What's happening...

Fear, what do you have to say?

Belief, what do you have to say?

Curiosity, what do you have to say?

Courage, what do you have to say?

Love, what do you have to say?

DATE : _____

What's happening...

Fear, what do you have to say?

Belief, what do you have to say?

Curiosity, what do you have to say?

_____
_____
_____
_____
_____
_____

Courage, what do you have to say?

_____
_____
_____
_____
_____
_____

Love, what do you have to say?

_____
_____
_____
_____
_____
_____

DATE : _____

What's happening...

Fear, what do you have to say?

Belief, what do you have to say?

Curiosity, what do you have to say?

Courage, what do you have to say?

Love, what do you have to say?

DATE : _____

What's happening...

Fear, what do you have to say?

Belief, what do you have to say?

Curiosity, what do you have to say?

Courage, what do you have to say?

Love, what do you have to say?

DATE : _____

I love myself enough to... Not give up after my first attempt if it didn't go the way I wanted first time.

Reflections...

DATE : _____

What's happening...

Fear, what do you have to say?

Belief, what do you have to say?

Curiosity, what do you have to say?

Courage, what do you have to say?

Love, what do you have to say?

DATE : _____

What's happening...

Fear, what do you have to say?

Belief, what do you have to say?

Curiosity, what do you have to say?

Courage, what do you have to say?

Love, what do you have to say?

DATE : _____

What's happening...

Fear, what do you have to say?

Belief, what do you have to say?

Curiosity, what do you have to say?

_____
_____
_____
_____
_____

Courage, what do you have to say?

_____
_____
_____
_____
_____

Love, what do you have to say?

_____
_____
_____
_____
_____

DATE : _____

What's happening...

Fear, what do you have to say?

Belief, what do you have to say?

Curiosity, what do you have to say?

_____
_____
_____
_____
_____
_____

Courage, what do you have to say?

_____
_____
_____
_____
_____
_____

Love, what do you have to say?

_____
_____
_____
_____
_____
_____

DATE : _____

What's happening...

Fear, what do you have to say?

Belief, what do you have to say?

Curiosity, what do you have to say?

Courage, what do you have to say?

Love, what do you have to say?

DATE : _____

I love myself enough to...
Do the thing that scares me.

Reflections...

DATE : _____

What's happening...

Fear, what do you have to say?

Belief, what do you have to say?

Curiosity, what do you have to say?

Courage, what do you have to say?

Love, what do you have to say?

DATE : _____

What's happening...

_____
_____
_____
_____
_____
_____

Fear, what do you have to say?

_____
_____
_____
_____
_____
_____

Belief, what do you have to say?

_____
_____
_____
_____
_____
_____

Curiosity, what do you have to say?

_____
_____
_____
_____
_____
_____

Courage, what do you have to say?

_____
_____
_____
_____
_____
_____

Love, what do you have to say?

_____
_____
_____
_____
_____
_____

DATE : _____

What's happening...

Fear, what do you have to say?

Belief, what do you have to say?

Curiosity, what do you have to say?

Courage, what do you have to say?

Love, what do you have to say?

DATE : _____

What's happening...

Fear, what do you have to say?

Belief, what do you have to say?

Curiosity, what do you have to say?

Courage, what do you have to say?

Love, what do you have to say?

DATE : _____

What's happening...

Fear, what do you have to say?

Belief, what do you have to say?

Curiosity, what do you have to say?

Courage, what do you have to say?

Love, what do you have to say?

DATE : _____

I love myself enough to... Stop second guessing myself and instead listen to my own intuition.

Reflections...

DATE : _____

What's happening...

Fear, what do you have to say?

Belief, what do you have to say?

Curiosity, what do you have to say?

_____
_____
_____
_____
_____
_____

Courage, what do you have to say?

_____
_____
_____
_____
_____
_____

Love, what do you have to say?

_____
_____
_____
_____
_____
_____

DATE : _____

What's happening...

Fear, what do you have to say?

Belief, what do you have to say?

Curiosity, what do you have to say?

Courage, what do you have to say?

Love, what do you have to say?

DATE : _____

What's happening...

Fear, what do you have to say?

Belief, what do you have to say?

Curiosity, what do you have to say?

Courage, what do you have to say?

Love, what do you have to say?

DATE : _____

What's happening...

Fear, what do you have to say?

Belief, what do you have to say?

Curiosity, what do you have to say?

_____
_____
_____
_____
_____
_____

Courage, what do you have to say?

_____
_____
_____
_____
_____
_____

Love, what do you have to say?

_____
_____
_____
_____
_____
_____

DATE : _____

What's happening...

Fear, what do you have to say?

Belief, what do you have to say?

Curiosity, what do you have to say?

Courage, what do you have to say?

Love, what do you have to say?

DATE : _____

I love myself enough to...
Never let my fears hold me back.

Reflections...

DATE : _____

Printed in Great Britain
by Amazon